GOD'S WORD
IN MY HEART

Books in My Time with God series

My Time with God

God's Word in My Heart

GOD'S WORD IN MY HEART

Paul J. Loth

Illustrated by
Daniel J. Hochstatter

THOMAS NELSON PUBLISHERS

Nashville

Published in Nashville, Tennessee, by Oliver-Nelson Books, a division of Thomas Nelson, Inc., Publishers, and distributed in Canada by Word Communications, Ltd., Richmond, British Columbia.

The Bible version used in this publication is the Contemporary English Version. Copyright © 1991, by the American Bible Society. Scripture noted NKJV is from THE NEW KING JAMES VERSION. Copyright © 1979, 1980, 1982, Thomas Nelson, Inc., Publishers.

Printed in the United States of America.

Library of Congress Cataloging in-Publication Data

Loth, Paul.
     God's word in my heart / Paul J. Loth.
         p.   cm.
     Summary: A collection of simple devotional readings offering lessons on basic Bible doctrines, using the three activities of thinking, learning, and praying.
     ISBN 0-8407-9233-6 (hard)
     1. Children—Prayer -books and devotionals—English   [1. Prayer books and devotionals.]   I. Title.
BV4571.2.L68   1993
242'.62—dc20   93-18774
                                                                                                         CIP
                                                                                                         AC

1 2 3 4 5 6 7 — 98 97 96 95 94 93

CONTENTS

An Open Letter to Children

You are special. God chose you to be His child. He wants you to spend time with Him.

Spending time with God is called having devotions. You read the Bible and pray.

This book teaches you what the Bible says about being God's child. It explains how to make God happy.

Find a quiet time to be alone with God. It helps if this is the same time each day. Find a place where no one will disturb you.

Each devotion in this book has three parts. Each part is important.

Think This section asks you to think about your life. Then the Bible lesson will be easier to understand.

Learn Each devotion teaches you a new lesson from the Bible. It shows you how to be a child of God.

Pray Learning something can be easy. But doing something about it can be hard. Praying helps you be a better Christian.

At the end of each devotion is a special verse from the Bible. You might want to memorize this verse.

I hope this book helps you get to know God in a wonderful way.

Paul J. Loth, Ed.D.

Answering Our Friends

Luke 5:27–39

Think When was the last time someone asked you to explain your actions?
What did you say?

Learn The Bible tells us we should act like Jesus. God sent the Holy Spirit to help us.

Jesus did not act like other people. People asked Him why He acted different.

We should act like Jesus. Our friends will ask why we act that way. We can tell them. It is because we love Jesus.

Pray Make me brave enough to act like Jesus.

Honor Christ and let him be the Lord of your life.
Always be ready to give an answer
when someone asks you about your hope.

1 Peter 3:15

Doing Our Job

Acts 20:17–38

Think   When was the last time you had a job to do?

Learn   Jesus has a job for us. It is to tell our friends about Him. That is what Jesus wants us to do.

Paul told people about Jesus. Paul did his job. He told many people about Jesus.

Our job is to tell our friends about Jesus. It is up to them to trust in Him.

Pray Please help me tell my friends about Jesus.

I have told you everything that God wants you to know.

Acts 20:27

Getting Help from God

John 16:7–15

Think Have you told your friends why you believe in Jesus?

What did they say?

Learn Jesus sent us a helper. The helper is the Holy Spirit.

The Holy Spirit helps us. He helps when we talk to our friends. He will help us know what to say. He helps us tell them about Jesus.

We must ask the Holy Spirit for help. We do this by praying. The Holy Spirit will help us.

Pray May the Holy Spirit help me talk to a friend.

The Spirit will come and show the people
of this world the truth.

John 16:8

Getting Help from God in Prayer

Romans 8:26–28

Think Do you always know the right thing to say?

Learn Sometimes we don't know what to pray for. We need help.

God helps us remember what to pray for.

We need to listen to God when we pray. Then we will be sure to pray for the right things.

Pray Help me to know what to pray for.

In certain ways we are weak,
but the Spirit is here to help us.
Romans 8:26

17

A Good Testimony

Acts 26

Think Have you ever told a friend about Jesus? What did you say?

Learn Paul knew about the Bible. He became a Christian. He told people about Jesus.

Paul told what Jesus did for him. He said that Jesus helped him each day.

We can tell our friends what Jesus does for us.

Pray   What can I tell my friends that Jesus has done for me? Please show me.

We cannot keep quiet about what we
have seen and heard.

Acts 4:20

Helping Jesus, Our Friend

Matthew 28:16–20; Mark 16:14–20

Think If your friends asked you to help them, what would you do? Why?

Learn Jesus is our best friend. We like to help our friends.

Jesus asked His friends to help Him. He told them to tell others about Him. They went all over the world. Jesus was pleased.

Jesus wants our help, too. We can tell people about Jesus.

Pray Show me whom I can tell about Jesus this week.

Go and preach the good news to everyone in the world.

Mark 16:15

Helping Our Friends
Love Jesus

1 Corinthians 8

Think How do you help your friends?

Are your friends better or worse because of your friendship?

Learn In Paul's time there was a problem. People had different ideas about right and wrong.

What should they do?

Paul taught them a lesson. They were not to do anything that would hurt another person. If they kept this in mind they would know right from wrong.

This is still right.

Pray   Show me how to help a friend walk closer to Jesus.

I am willing to put up with anything.
Then God's special people will be saved.

2 Timothy 2:10

Letting the Bible Speak for Us

Acts 2:14–39; 13:13–41

(**Think**)   How do you decide whom to believe when you and your friends disagree?

Is one of your friends always right?

(**Learn**)   Sometimes we do not know how to tell about Jesus. The disciples did. They told what the Bible said. It tells about Jesus.

Paul told people about Jesus. Paul knew verses from the Bible. The verses told about Jesus.

We can tell friends about Jesus. We can tell them what the Bible says. It tells about Jesus.

Pray   Help me learn Bible verses to share with a friend.

My word . . . shall accomplish what I please.

Isaiah 55:11, NKJV

Praying for Unsaved Friends

John 14—16

Think When was the last time you had trouble doing something?

Did you ask for help?

Learn We may need help telling our friends about Jesus. We can tell them what Jesus means to us. But they still do not trust in Jesus. God can help our friends to trust Jesus.

God can help our friends understand about Jesus. We can also help our friends. We can pray for them. It will help.

Pray Help my friends understand about Jesus.

God is patient, because he wants everyone to turn from sin.

2 Peter 3:9

Sharing Our Experiences

John 9:1–34

Think When something good happens to you, do you want to tell someone?

Whom do you tell?

Learn A man could not see. He had always been blind.

One day Jesus helped the man see. He was very happy.

He told the people what Jesus did for him.

We can tell our friends how Jesus helps us, too. This is how we share about Jesus.

Pray Show me how to share ways You have helped me.

All I know is that I used to be blind, but now I can see!

John 9:25

Standing Up for God

Exodus 32; Acts 4—5

Think When has a friend stood up for you? How did you feel?

Learn Moses stood up for God. He spoke to the people. He said to worship only God.

Peter told about Jesus. Some leaders told him to be quiet. But he was not. He stood up for Jesus.

We can stand up for Jesus, too. We can be like Moses and Peter.

Pray Help me to be strong and brave for You.

If you tell others that you belong to me, I will tell my
father in heaven that you are my followers.

Matthew 10:32

Telling Our Friends
We Love Them

John 13:34–35; Philippians 1:3–8; 1 Thessalonians 2:19–20

Think When was the last time someone told you they loved you?

How did you feel?

Learn People can tell we love Jesus. We should be kind to one another. Then people will know that we love Jesus.

Paul did more than that. He told his friends he loved them. He showed them he loved them.

We should show our friends that we love them. God likes it when we love each other.

Pray Help me tell my friends I love them.

If you love each other, everyone will know
you are my disciples.
John 13:35

Using Our Opportunities

Acts 8:26–39

Think Have you ever had a chance to do something you really wanted to do?

How did you feel?

Learn Philip saw a man reading the Bible. The man did not understand what he was reading. Philip told him. Philip told him about Jesus.

God gave Philip a chance. Philip used his chance. He told about Jesus.

God gives us chances, too. We should be ready. We can tell what Jesus means to us.

Pray   Give me a chance to tell a friend about Jesus.

We are telling you what we have seen and heard, so that you may share in this life with us.

1 John 1:3

35

Getting the Point Across

Luke 11:5–8

Think When was the last time you had a hard time getting your point across to your parents?
What did you do?

Learn God loves us. He wants what is best for us. He will give us what we need.

Jesus told a story: A friend knocks on our door. It is the middle of the night. "Let me borrow some food," he says. We say, "Go away." He keeps knocking. Finally, we get the food.

Jesus explained the story. If we would help a friend, God will surely give us what we need.

Pray Give me the faith to keep praying.

So I tell you to ask and you will receive.

Luke 11:9

A Picture of a Prayer Warrior

Matthew 4:1–11; Luke 6:12–16; 22:39–46

Think Whom do you know who prays a lot? When does that person pray?

Learn Jesus prayed about many things. He prayed about His friends. He prayed the night before He died.

Jesus asked God what to do. He listened to what God told Him. God helped Him do the right thing.

Pray Help me pray every day this week.

Never stop praying.

1 Thessalonians 5:17

A Picture Perfect Prayer

Luke 11:2–4

Think How do you learn something new?

Learn Jesus showed us how to pray. We can copy Him.

Jesus prayed the Lord's Prayer. This special prayer teaches us how to pray.

We should praise God. Next, ask Him to forgive our sins. Then we can ask God to help us.

Pray Help me to learn how to pray.

Morning, noon, and night, you hear my
concerns and my complaints.
Psalm 55:17

Pray and Believe

Matthew 21:20–22

Think Have you ever asked for something that you did not really believe you would get?

Learn God loves us. He will do what is best for us. When we ask God for things, we can believe this.

God will answer our prayers. Jesus said we must have faith. If we have faith, we can tell a mountain to move. It will move!

When we have faith, we can pray and God will answer us.

Pray   Let me have faith when I pray to You.

If you have faith when you pray, you will be given
whatever you ask for.

Matthew 21:22

Pray, Do Not Worry

Matthew 6:25–34

Think   Have you ever seen a bird starve to death? Why not?

Who takes care of the birds?

Learn   God takes care of everything. He cares for all the birds. He cares for the flowers.

But God loves people even more. More than flowers. More than birds.

Jesus told us not to worry. God will take care of us. We just have to ask Him. Instead of worrying, we can pray. God knows everything we need. All we need to do is talk to Him.

Pray   Help me to not worry but to trust You for all I need.

Don't worry about anything, but pray for everything.

Philippians 4:6

Prayer Works

Acts 12:1–19

Think When you really want something, what do you do?

Learn One day Peter was talking about Jesus. He was put in jail. The Christians loved Peter. They wanted to help him. What could they do?

They could pray. They asked God to help Peter. God heard their prayer. He sent angels. Peter was freed.

They learned a lesson. Prayer works!

Pray When I am worried, help me remember to pray.

The prayer of an innocent person is powerful.

James 5:16

Praying for Others

Acts 20:17–38; Ephesians 6:18–20; Philippians 1:3–11

Think Have you ever wanted to help someone but did not know what to do?

What is the best way to help your friends?

Learn Paul asked people to pray for him. Paul prayed that God would help his friends live for God.

Paul said goodbye to his friends in Ephesus. Paul did something special with these friends. He prayed for them. He asked God to take care of them.

We can do that with our friends, too. The best way we can help our friends is to pray for them.

Pray   I pray for all the friends on my prayer list. Please take care of them.

Never give up praying.

Colossians 4:2

Praying with Our Friends

Acts 1:9–26

Think When was the last time you prayed with someone else?

How was it different from praying alone?

Learn Jesus was gone to heaven. The disciples were together. They were in the upper room. Jesus told them to wait there.

What did they do while they waited? They prayed. Everyone prayed to God. They prayed together.

God wants us to pray together, too. We can pray with our friends. This is a good way for friends to show they care.

(Pray) Help me to pray with my friends
this week.

I want everyone everywhere to lift innocent hands
toward heaven and pray.

1 Timothy 2:8

Thanking God in Prayer

Luke 18:35–42

Think   When someone does something nice for you, what do you say?
Why?

Learn   Jesus healed a man who was blind. What do you think the man said? Right. He said thank You. He praised Jesus. This pleased Jesus.

God wants us to thank Him, too. When we pray, God answers our prayers. He wants us to remember to thank Him.

Pray I thank You for Your love, and for all You give me.

It is wonderful to be grateful and to sing your praises, LORD most high!

Psalm 92:1

Using Prayer to Praise God

Ephesians 1

Think Do you listen when someone prays in church?

Why do people pray out loud?

Learn The Psalms give praise to God. Many of the psalms are prayers to God.

God likes to hear that we love Him. We can tell Him that when we pray.

When we pray in church, we praise God. Church services are good times to praise God together.

Pray   You are good. You are great. Help me to praise You.

I will praise you each day and always honor your name.

Psalm 145:2

Changing Our Reflections

James 1:21–26

Think What do you see when you look in the mirror?

Learn We should all read our Bibles. It shows us if we are obeying God.

Some people read the Bible. But they do not change. That is like looking in a mirror and forgetting what you see.

We should do what the Bible says. Then we are obeying God.

Pray Let me be changed by reading the Bible.

Obey God's message! Don't fool yourselves
by just listening to it.

James 1:22

Keeping God's Word

Psalm 119:11

Think Do you have trouble remembering important things?

How do you do it?

Learn We do not always have our Bible with us. How do we know what it says? We can memorize parts of it. Then we can think about it anytime.

David memorized the Bible. He did it so he would not sin.

We can do the same thing. The more we know, the more it will help us.

Pray Help me learn Your word by heart.

I treasure your word above all else; it keeps me
from sinning against you.

Psalm 119:11

Learning About God

Acts 2:42, 17:10–13; Romans 10:1–4

Think How do you learn about God?

When was the last time you learned something about God? What was it?

Learn Church is important. It is one place we learn about God. We learn what Jesus taught.

The first Christians were taught by the apostles. They taught from the Scriptures. They taught what Jesus had said. The Christians wanted to learn more about God.

We learn from the Bible. We learn from teachers. We learn from prayer and songs.

Pray Help me learn more about Jesus
in church.

Make me wise enough to learn what you have commanded.

Psalm 119:73

Letting the Bible Explain Itself

Luke 4:16–21; Acts 2:14–36; Galatians 4:21–31

Think What do you do if someone says something you do not understand?

Learn A verse may be hard to understand. We have all had this problem.

Here is something we can do. We can look for other verses on the same subject. Then we read them, too. This will help.

We may want to learn about prayer. So we read many verses. This will make it clearer.

Pray Give me understanding. Help me to know Your word.

Help me understand your teachings.

Psalm 119:27

Telling Us How to Live

2 Timothy 3:1–17

Think How do you know what you are to do? Who tells you the rules to follow?

Learn Rules help us. They tell us how to live. Our rule book is the Bible.

Paul wanted to help Timothy know how to live. He told him to study the Bible. The Bible would help him know what to do.

The Bible will help us do the right thing, too. Knowing it will help us know how to live for Christ.

Pray Help me to live as the Bible tells me.

Your word to me, your servant, is like pure gold.

Psalm 119:140

Telling Us What to Believe

2 Timothy 3

Think If you wanted to find out the truth, what would you do?

How do you know whom to believe?

Learn Paul told Timothy to expect hard times. The years would be tough. Paul wanted Timothy to be ready.

Timothy had been taught the Bible. Paul wanted him to keep reading the Bible. Then he would know what was right. The Bible would tell him what to believe.

We learn the same way.

Pray When I am unsure about what to believe, help me find the answer in the Bible.

I will take pleasure in your laws
and remember your word.

Psalm 119:16

Being a Giver in the Church

Acts 4:32–37

Think Tell about a time you gave something to someone.

How did you feel?

Learn Jesus watched people give. One lady gave two coins. Jesus said, "She gave more than the others. She gave all she had."

We can give to God. We can give at church.

Some people are good at giving. They help the church. We should be givers, too.

(**Pray**) Help me give to others.

God loves people who love to give.

2 Corinthians 9:7

Being a Helper in the Church

Acts 6:1–7

(**Think**) Whom do you know who always helps others?

(**Learn**) The apostles needed help. They chose some helpers. Now they had more time to tell about Jesus.

Helping is easy for some people. All of us should try to help. Jesus would like that.

Pray Show me how to help someone at church.

Serve each other with love.

Galatians 5:13

Being a Leader in the Church

Romans 12:8; Ephesians 4:11–16

Think Do your friends always seem to follow what one person wants?

Learn Leaders in the Bible help others follow God. Jesus was the best leader of all.

God gives the church people to lead it.

Leaders help us do the right thing.

Our church has leaders. They help us serve God. We can be leaders, too.

Pray   Show me how I can be a leader right now.

Christ chose some of us to be apostles, prophets,
missionaries, pastors, and teachers.

Ephesians 4:11–12

Being a Teacher

Romans 12:3–8; James 3:1

Think Who taught you about God?
What special teachers do you know in the church?

Learn People in the church teach us about God. We can teach our friends about God, too.

James said teachers should teach right things. They should be careful to teach God's truth.

God gave teachers to help us. They help us learn about God.

Pray Thank You for those who teach me about You.

I want you to tell these same things to followers who can be trusted to tell others.

2 Timothy 2:2

Being an Encourager

Acts 4:36–37; 14:21–15:35

Think Whom do you know who encourages you?

Learn Barnabas was Paul's friend. He encouraged Paul.

He made Paul feel better.

Barnabas did a good job. He was an encourager. We can encourage our friends. Our friends will feel better. We will feel good, too.

Pray Let me be good at making people feel better.

Encourage and help each other.

1 Thessalonians 5:11

The Church Is Family

1 Corinthians 12:12–31

Think How many members do you have in your family?

How does your family take care of each other?

Learn The church is like our body. Our body has many parts. Each part is different. But each part is important.

The church is God's family.

Our family is like our body. Each of us has a job to do. We have a job to do in the church, too. We help each other. This is what it means to be in God's family.

Pray   Help me to serve my church family.

There are many of us, but we each are part of
the body of Christ.

Romans 12:5

Giving to God

Luke 21:1–4

Think Do you give an offering at church? Why?

Learn God is happy when we give to Him. It shows that we love Him.

Once Jesus watched people give offerings. A poor woman gave two small coins. Jesus was pleased. She gave all she had. Others gave what they did not need. The poor woman loved Jesus.

We can give offerings too. This shows that we love God. This pleases God.

Pray Show me what offering to give at church next Sunday.

You will be blessed in every way, and you will be able to keep on being generous.

2 Corinthians 9:11

Listening to God

1 Samuel 3:1–10

Think Have you ever tried talking with someone who doesn't answer?

Did you have trouble?

Learn Samuel was a young boy. He worked in the temple. Samuel heard God speak to him.

Samuel listened. God told Samuel all the plans He had for him.

God will talk to us, too. He calls us inside where only we can hear Him. The next time that happens, we should listen carefully.

Pray This week, help me listen to what You say.

Listen, my people, while I, the Lord, correct you!

Psalm 81:8

83

Worshiping God Through Music

Psalm 150

Think What songs do you like to sing at church?

How do you think God feels when you sing songs about Him?

Learn King David wrote songs. He wrote about God. People sang these songs in worship. They used them to praise God.

God enjoys it when we sing. Many songs use words from the Bible. The choir sings. Instruments play. Everyone sings to God. God likes that.

We can worship God with music. God will listen.

Pray   Thank You for the joy of singing to You!

Shout praises to the LORD! Sing him a new song of praise when his loyal people meet.

Psalm 149:1

Worshiping Together

Psalms 147—149

Think Do you like to do things alone or with others?
Why?

Learn God wants us to worship Him.

We do not worship God by ourselves. We do it with other people.

It is good to worship God with our friends. We can help each other. It is good to have friends to help us worship God.

(**Pray**) Make me glad to worship You
with others!

When your people meet, you will fill my heart
with your praises, LORD.

Psalm 22:25

Attendance Is Required

Acts 2:40–47

Think Is there something that you have to attend? Do you like to go?

Learn It is hard to be a Christian. Jesus knew it would be. That is why Jesus gave us churches.

The first Christians spent a lot of time together. They learned about God. They talked with each other. They prayed. They sang hymns.

We should spend time in church. It is good to be with others who believe as we do. We can help each other learn.

Pray Thank You for giving me my church.

Some people have gotten out of the habit of meeting for worship, but we must not do that.

Hebrews 10:25

The Battle Is the Lord's

2 Chronicles 20

Think Has anyone else ever taken care of one of your problems?

What happened?

Learn Israel was fighting a strong enemy. They were scared. They prayed about it. "Go out and fight," God told them. "I have already won the battle for you."

So Israel fought.

And they won!

God helps us every day, too. When we have a problem, God will help us. He will take care of us. What could be better than having God on our side?

Pray Help me with my problems. Help me know that You take care of me.

The battle is not yours, but God's.

2 Chronicles 20:15, NKJV

Doing Our Best for Jesus

Matthew 5:16; 1 Corinthians 10:31

Think What are some jobs you have done in the last week?

Did you do your best?

Learn Paul always did his best. He studied hard. He worked hard. He told people about Jesus. People knew he loved God.

We do all things to the glory of God.

We should always do our best. Then people will know we love God.

Pray Help me to do my best on the job.

Make your light shine, so that others will see the good
that you do and will praise your Father in heaven.

Matthew 5:16

93

Enjoying God

Genesis 1; Luke 18:15–17

Think When was the last time you enjoyed spending time with someone?

Learn God wanted friends. So God made human beings. They enjoyed each other.

Children enjoyed being with Jesus. They had a good time together.

We can have a good time with God, too. We can enjoy God.

Pray Help me spend more time with You.

So Jesus called the children over to him and said, "Let the children come to me!"

Luke 18:16

Following God's Plan

Genesis 12: 21–22

Think When you play with your friends, who decides what to do?

Learn God had a plan. He told Abraham and Sarah they would have a child.

God gave them a son. He was named Isaac.

They had followed God's plan. This pleased God.

We need to follow God's plan, too.

(**Pray**)   Do You have a plan for me to follow right now?

But what the LORD has planned will stand forever.

Psalm 33:11

Following Jesus

Matthew 4:18–22; John 13:1–20

Think Whom do you admire?
Do you try to copy that person?

Learn Jesus had some helpers. They were His disciples. They followed Him.

Jesus taught them how to act. He taught by example. Jesus served others. He taught them to serve others.

We can follow Jesus, too. We will learn how to act. This will help us be like Jesus. This will please Jesus.

Pray I want to live the way Jesus lived. I need Your help.

Always live as God's holy people should.

1 Peter 1:15

Keeping God on Our Minds

Colossians 3:1–4

Think   What do you think about when you're doing nothing else?

Learn   Paul was in prison. He was still happy. How could that be?

Paul wrote letters while he was in prison. He explained why he was happy. He was thinking about Jesus. This made him happy.

This will work for us, too. We need to keep our minds on Jesus. Our problems won't seem so bad.

Pray Help me to keep my mind on Jesus.

Think about what is up there,
not about what is here on earth.

Colossians 3:2

101

Keeping Our Minds on Good Things

Philippians 4

Think What do you like to think about? Does what you think about affect how you act?

Learn Christians in the early church had problems. People were mad at them. They were put into jail. Some were killed.

These were big problems. They thought about them all the time. It made it hard to do the right things.

Paul told the Christians to think about good things. Their minds would be filled with good things. They would be much happier.

Pray Help me think about good things this week.

Keep your minds on whatever is true,
pure, right, holy, friendly, and proper.

Philippians 4:8

Knowing God's Will

Psalm 119:105

[Think] What is the best way to find out what someone is thinking?

[Learn] We want to obey God. But how can we know what God wants us to do? We learn what to do when we pray and listen to Him. We listen by reading the Bible.

The Bible "is a lamp to my feet and light to my path." It will show us God's will.

We should read the Bible and pray to God. This will help us know God's will.

Pray Help me read my Bible every day.

Your word is a lamp that gives light wherever I walk.

Psalm 119:105

Looking at Jesus

Matthew 14:22–33

Think When have you been somewhere very high in the sky?

Were you scared?

Learn Peter saw Jesus walking on the water.

Jesus called, "Come." Peter was able to walk on the water, too. He was looking at Jesus. But Peter looked away from Jesus. He started to sink. Jesus saved him.

When Peter stopped looking at Jesus, he sank.

We should look at Jesus, too. Then we can do great things.

Pray When I am scared, help me think of You.

We must keep our eyes on Jesus, who leads us and makes
our faith complete.

Hebrews 12:2

Loving God

Mark 12:28–34; John 14:21–24

Think How do you treat people you love? How do you know that people love you?

Learn Loving God is important. We should love Him with all our hearts.

If we love God, we will obey Him. The disciples loved God. They wanted to obey Him.

We love God, too. We want Him to be happy. We make God happy by obeying Him. This shows we love God.

Pray What have I done to show You that I love You?

If anyone loves me, they will obey me.

John 14:23

Making God Number One

Mark 10:17–22

Think Who is your favorite friend? What does that mean?

Learn A rich man asked a question: "What do I need to do to be saved?"

"What does the Bible say?" Jesus asked.

"Love the Lord with all your heart," the man said. "And love your neighbor as yourself."

"Right," Jesus said. "Sell everything you own. Come and follow Me."

The man was sad. He would not do this. Jesus was sad, too.

Pray   Let Jesus be the most important thing in my life.

But more than anything else, put God's work first.

Matthew 6:33

111

Making Our Goal

1 Corinthians 9:15–27

Think Have you ever tried to talk to someone that did not seem to understand you?

Learn Paul loved Jesus. He told people about Jesus. That was his goal.

Paul talked to everyone. He wanted them to listen. He did not let things get in his way. He had a goal.

We should tell our friends about Jesus. That should be our goal.

Pray Show me how to reach my friends
for Jesus.

I do everything I can to win everyone I possibly can.

1 Corinthians 9:22

113

Obeying God

Exodus 19—20

Think Do you like rules? Why? Why not? Why are there rules?

Learn God told Moses to come to the top of the mountain.

God said to Moses, "I am the Lord your God. I freed you from slavery. You will be My people."

God gave Moses rules. The people would obey. They knew God wanted what was best for them.

God wants us to obey His rules, too. God will be happy. Then we will be happy, too.

Pray   Let me obey the rules God has given.

Direct me by your command! I love to do what you say.

Psalm 119:35

Telling God "Thank You"

Luke 17:11–19

Think When someone does something nice for you, what do you do?

Learn Psalms is filled with songs to God. It was the first hymn book. Many psalms say "thank you" to God.

God likes it when we thank Him. Then He knows that we like what He did.

Jesus helped many people. Most people thanked Him. One time Jesus healed ten sick people. Only one thanked Him. This made Jesus sad.

Pray   Thank You for all You have done for me.

Our God, we thank you for being so near to us! Everyone celebrates your wonderful deeds.

Psalm 75:1

Telling God We Are Sorry

John 18:15–27; 21:15–19

(Think) How do you feel when you've done something wrong?

What makes you feel better?

(Learn) Peter was sad. He had let Jesus down. Peter had lied. He had said he did not know Jesus.

Soon Peter saw Jesus. He said he was sorry. He asked Jesus to forgive Him. Jesus did.

Jesus will forgive us, too. We have to tell Him we are sorry.

Pray Please forgive me for the wrong things I do.

But if we confess our sins to God, he can always be trusted to forgive us and take our sins away.

1 John 1:9

Waiting for God

Exodus 3, 14

Think How do you feel when you have to wait for something?

Learn The Israelites were slaves. They asked God to save them. God told them to wait. Then He sent Moses to save them.

Moses led the people out of Egypt. They had to wait, but God saved them.

God has plans for us. We may have to wait to see what they are.

Pray Help me to trust You even when I have
to wait.

Be brave and strong and trust the Lord.

Psalm 27:14

121

Worshiping God Alone

Exodus 19; John 6:15

Think When was the last time you wanted to be alone?

What did you do?

Learn Jesus spent time alone with God. Moses spent time alone with God. This pleased God.

Jesus prayed. And God told Jesus what to do.

Moses listened to God also. Then Moses knew what to tell the people.

We can spend time alone with God, too. We can tell God that we love Him.

(Pray) Help me listen when You speak to
my heart.

Pray to your Father in private.

Matthew 6:6

123

Encouraging Others

Acts 4:36; 12:25—13:3

Think   How do you make your friends feel when you're with them?

Learn   Paul had friends to encourage him. This helped Paul. It kept him going.

It is easy to be discouraged. We need friends to encourage us.

We want to encourage our friends. This helps them want to do the right thing. This pleases God.

Pray   Teach me how to encourage my friends.

Encourage and help each other.

1 Thessalonians 5:11

Forgiving and Forgetting

Matthew 18:21–35

Think When was the last time someone did something wrong to you?

Learn A man owed a lot of money. The man he owed did not make him pay. He was forgiven. The man who was forgiven was owed a small amount. He made the one who owed him pay.

The first man was not fair. He was treated well. He should treat others well, too.

God forgives us for what we do. We should forgive and forget.

Pray   Help me forgive my friends.

If you forgive others for the wrongs they do to you, your
Father in heaven will forgive you.

Matthew 6:14

127

Giving Up Our Rights

Philippians 2:6–11

Think   When was a time someone tried to take advantage of you?

What did you do?

Learn   Jesus always obeyed God. He even gave up His own rights in order to obey.

Jesus was dying on the cross. Some soldiers made fun of Him. What did Jesus do? He did not try to get even. He asked God to forgive them.

We should obey God, too. It may mean giving up our own rights. This is a small price to pay to obey God.

Pray Show me how to act when people are mean to me.

But I tell you to love your enemies and pray
for anyone who mistreats you.

Matthew 5:44

Helping Others

Acts 9:1–19

Think   Have you ever helped someone who was not nice to you?

Learn   Before Paul loved Jesus, he was mean.

Jesus asked Paul for help. Then Paul loved Jesus, too. He was not mean.

God told a man to help Paul. The man was scared of Paul. He knew Paul had been mean.

God says we should help everyone. Even someone who has been mean.

Pray   I want to help people this week. Please show me how.

Use your [freedom] as an opportunity
to serve each other with love.

Galatians 5:13

Helping Others Live

2 Timothy 3:1–17

Think Have you ever tried to tell someone they are doing something wrong?

Learn The Bible is God's Word. God uses it to show people when they are doing wrong things.

Timothy had to tell people they were doing wrong things. He used the Bible to do this.

Paul said the Bible helps people stop doing wrong things. It helps them know the right thing.

The Bible helps us, too. It shows us how to do the right thing.

Pray How can I help someone do the right thing?

Understanding your word gives light to the minds of ordinary people.

Psalm 119:130

Looking Out for Others

John 6:1–14; Philippians 2:1–4

Think How do you try to help your friends? Do you help them even if it is hard for you?

Learn Jesus cared about others. Many people came to hear Him. Jesus gave them all food. He showed He cared.

We should care, too. Jesus wants us all to get along. We should not just think of ourselves. We should be like Jesus.

What would happen if we all did that? The world would be better. Right?

Pray Help me think of others before I think of myself.

Care about them as much as you care about yourselves.

Philippians 2:4

Loyalty to the End

Genesis 1; Exodus 4; 1 Samuel 20; John 15:13–15; Acts 4—6

Think Who are some of your closest friends? Would they be loyal to you no matter what?

Learn God wants us to have friends. God is happy when we are good friends to others.

The Bible tells us about many good friends. They helped each other. This made God happy.

The best friend of all is Jesus. He gave His life for us. He will do anything for us. We should try to be that kind of friend, too.

Pray Make me a better friend to someone today.

A true friend is closer than your own family.

Proverbs 18:24

Picking Friends

Genesis 37

Think How did you choose your friends?
When did any of your friends make you do something for which you were sorry?

Learn We read about many friends in the Bible. These friends helped each other. They helped each other do the right thing.

Bad friends get us in trouble. Joseph's brothers were not good friends. The brothers were mean to Joseph. They helped each other do the wrong thing.

We must choose good friends. Good friends help us do the right thing.

Pray Give me good friends who help me obey You.

Wise friends make you wise.

Proverbs 13:20

Sacrificing for Others

Luke 10:25–37

Think   When was the last time you gave up something to help a friend?

Learn   Jesus gave us two laws. First, love the Lord. Second, love your neighbor.

Giving up your life is real love. Jesus did that. He gave up His life for us.

Jesus told about a good man. He saw a hurt man by the road. He helped the man.

This is called sacrifice. Sacrifice is giving to help others. Sacrifice is part of love. It makes Jesus happy.

Pray Show me what I can sacrifice to help someone.

Children, you show love for others by truly helping them.

1 John 3:18

141

Serving Others

John 13:1–20

Think When was the last time you helped someone?

What did you do?

What is the best way you can help others?

Learn Many people do not like to serve others. But Jesus taught us to serve.

Jesus washed dirty feet. He served others. He taught us to serve.

We all have "gifts." These are things we are good at. We are to use our "gifts." We use them to serve others.

Pray   Help me to use my gifts to serve others.

If you want to be great, you must be the servant
of all the others.

Matthew 20:26

Sharing with Others

Acts 2:40–47

Think How do you feel when one of your friends is sad?

What do you do?

Learn The early Christians liked to be together. They shared with each other. They gave things to each other. They shared the good times. They also shared the bad times.

Peter and John were in jail. This was a bad time. All the people were sad. Soon they were set free. Then people were happy.

We can share with others, too. We can share with people in our church.

(Pray) Let me share something important with a friend.

When others are happy, be happy with them, and when they are sad, be sad.

Romans 12:15

145

Being Kind to Everyone

Matthew 5:38–42; Romans 12:9–21

Think What do you do when people are mean to you?

Learn We should be kind to everyone. Some people are not kind to us. We should even be kind to them.

Some people are not this way. They try to pay others back. Jesus does not like this. He does not want us to act this way. He wants us to obey Him.

If we obey, we are acting like Jesus. This makes Jesus happy.

Pray Help me be kind to those who are mean to me.

If your enemies are hungry, give them something to eat.

Proverbs 25:21–22

Praying for Those Who Do Mean Things

Matthew 5:43–48

Think Have you ever helped someone who was mean to you?

What did you do? Why?

Learn Life was hard for the first Christians. Some people hated Jesus. They were mean.

Jesus told the Christians what to do. He said, "Be kind to your enemies. Pray for those who are mean to you."

It worked. They prayed for their enemies. Then they did not act so mean. God helped the Christians to be nicer, too. We should do this, too.

Pray When people are mean, help me to pray for them.

Pray for those who spitefully use you and persecute you.

Matthew 5:44

Avoiding Bad Situations

Genesis 39

Think When have you had trouble doing the right thing? Why was it hard?

Learn Sometimes it is hard to do the right thing. Joseph loved God. One day it was hard for him to obey God. What could Joseph do?

Joseph ran away.

Then he could obey God.

Sometimes it is hard for us to obey God. But we can do what Joseph did. Run away!

Pray Keep me from places where I might do wrong.

Respect the LORD and stay away from evil.

Proverbs 3:7

Resisting Temptation

Genesis 39; Psalm 139–144; Matthew 4

Think When was the last time you thought about doing something wrong?

Did you do it? Why? Why not?

Learn How can we keep from doing the wrong thing?

When Joseph was tempted, he ran away. Sometimes that is best. We can play with other friends.

David was tempted to do wrong. He prayed.

When Jesus was tempted to do wrong, He quoted from the Bible.

God wants us to obey Him. We may need help to do the right thing. God will help if we ask Him.

Pray Help me when I am tempted to do
wrong.

God will show you how to escape from your temptations.

1 Corinthians 10:13

Using the Bible to Win

Luke 4:1–11

Think How do you know the right thing to do? Is it easy to always know what is right?

Learn Jesus was in the desert. He was tempted to do wrong. He used God's Word. It helped Him do the right thing.

The Bible is God's Word. The Bible will help us do the right thing. It can help us obey God.

Everyone is tempted to do wrong. We can use the Bible to win.

Pray Let the Bible guide me to obey You.

By your teachings, Lord, I am warned; by obeying them, I am greatly rewarded.

Psalm 19:11

Believing the Impossible

Exodus 5–14; Mark 9:1–29

(Think) What can you think of that would never happen?

(Learn) God does many things. Some do not seem possible. Once His people were trapped. They had to cross a sea. God split the water. His people were saved. It was a miracle.

Jesus did miracles, too. He healed the sick. He walked on water. God helped Jesus.

God can help us, too. There is nothing God cannot do.

Pray   I am thankful You can do miracles.

God can do anything.

Mark 10:27

Trusting God When We are Scared

Luke 8:22–25; Acts 16:16–34

Think When was the last time you were scared?

What did you do?

Learn The disciples were scared during a storm. They asked Jesus for help. Jesus stopped the storm.

Paul and Silas were in jail. They were scared. They sang songs to God. They had learned to trust in God.

Jesus' friends learned to trust Him. He would take care of them. God will take care of us, too.

Pray When I am scared, remind me to pray to You.

God is our mighty fortress, always ready to help
in times of trouble.

Psalm 46:1